Turn Your Chaos Into Calm

Bruno the Poodle's Quotes and Prompts to Reveal New Paths to Balance

BOOK III

J. J. Jordan

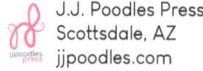

J.J. Poodles Press
Scottsdale, AZ
jjpoodles.com

Turn Your Chaos Into Calm, Book III of the Pocket Lifestyle Journal Series

Published by

J.J. Poodles Press
Scottsdale, AZ
jjpoodles.com

Copyright ©2021 J.J. Jordan. All rights reserved.

No part of this book may be reproduced or transmitted in any form or by any means, electronic or mechanical, including photocopying, recording, or by any information storage and retrieval system, without permission in writing from the copyright owner.

Scripture quotations marked (TLB) are taken from The Living Bible copyright © 1971. Used by permission of Tyndale House Publishers, Inc., Carol Stream, Illinois 60188. All rights reserved.

Scripture quotations marked TPT are from The Passion Translation®. Copyright © 2017, 2018 by Passion & Fire Ministries, Inc. Used by permission. All rights reserved. thePassionTranslation.com.

Cover Design by Angie Alaya of pro_ebookcovers

Interior Design by DocUmeantDesigns
www.DocUmeantDesigns.com

ISBN: 978-1-7340944-7-3

Contents

V	INTRODUCTION
1	PART 1: FUN & HUMOR
13	PART 2: LOVE
25	PART 3: SAFETY & SERENITYS
41	PART 4: SUCCESS & GOALS
57	PART 5: SELF-ESTEEM & SELF-LOVE

Introduction

2020. Ugh! One of the toughest, most unprecedented years in current history. A world-wide health crisis. Civil unrest. A divisive competition for the U.S. presidency. Even wild weather patterns.

As I watched the chaos in the world unfolding, and experienced its turbulent fallout in my immediate circle, I yearned for calm. I spoke with friends and family and found most searching for solace as well. And we are not alone. Many others, probably including you, reel with imbalance and are seeking for ways to cope.

This realization prompted me to create this book to serve you as a beautiful quiet eye in the hurricane of present-day life. Its inspirational quotes can help bring you back into balance and focus, no matter what happens to you or around you. It also provides areas to write down your goals, visions, and action items. Journaling—therapeutic in itself—can spark enlightened thoughts. These bring clarity and fresh ideas to create more harmony and joy in your experience. The more you do it, the easier it becomes, and the more the ideas flow.

I designed the book to provide inspiration, so don't feel like you need to use it from cover to cover. Pick and choose an area/topic to write about every day, or as the mood hits you. I encourage you to be patient with your progress, and to celebrate even the smallest accomplishment as you mindfully wind your way through the raging storm toward inner peace.

This first book will touch on the important topics of friends, relationships, spirituality, hope and meaning, health, nutrition, exercise, and career. At the beginning of each section is a Balance Wheel specific to the chapter. Think of your life as wheels. Are your wheels well-rounded and balanced? You can pick a section of the wheel that may need maintenance. Just like the wheels on your car need to be balanced and aligned, so does your life. This Journal will help you keep your life calm, chaos free, and in balance.

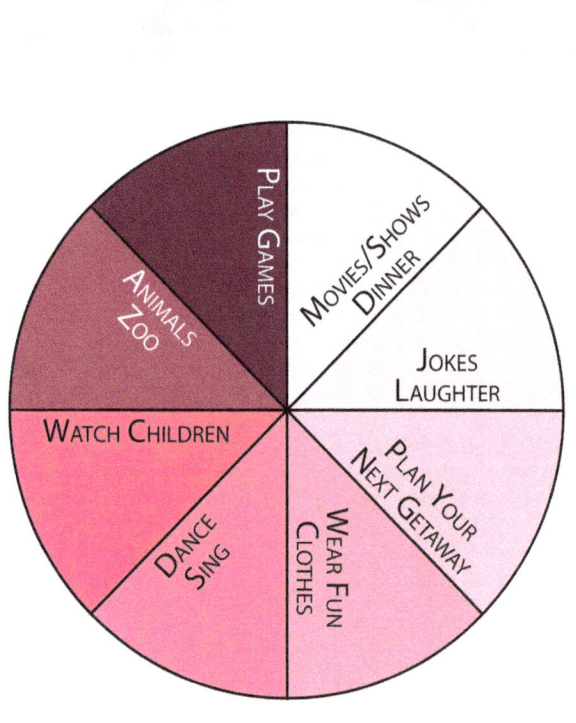

Part 1
Fun & Humor

"We don't stop playing because we grow old; we grow old because we stop playing." —George Bernard Shaw

Are you playing and having fun? How can you add play and fun to your life today?

_____
_____
_____
_____
_____
_____
_____
_____
_____
_____
_____
_____
_____
_____
_____
_____
_____

Action Plan & Goals

Have Fun & Stay in **Balance & Live Fully**.

I commit to:

"Do something just for fun. Pleasure is one of life's essential nutrients." —Cheryl Richardson

What are you doing for fun?

Action Plan & Goals
Have Fun & Stay in **Balance & Live Fully**.

I commit to:

"Life is far too important a thing ever to talk seriously about." —Oscar Wilde

Are you too serious?

Action Plan & Goals

Have Fun & Stay in **Balance & Live Fully**.

I commit to:

"If your ship doesn't come in, swim out to it!"
—Jonathan Winters 1925–2013

Where do you want to swim to?

Action Plan & Goals

Have Fun & Stay in **Balance & Live Fully**.

I commit to:

"Why not go out on a limb? Isn't that where the fruit is?"
—Frank Scully 1892–1964

In what way are you willing to go out on a limb?

Action Plan & Goals

Have Fun & Stay in **Balance & Live Fully**.

I commit to:

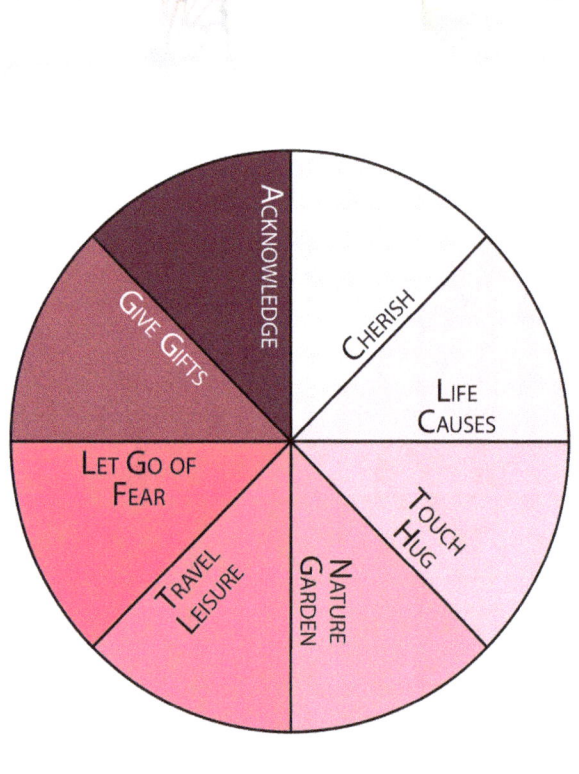

Part 2
Love

"Love your enemies, for they tell you your faults."
—Benjamin Franklin

Do you love your enemies and accept your faults?

Action Plan & Goals

Love More & Stay in **Balance & Live Fully**.

I commit to:

"The more you are motivated by love, the more fearless and free your actions will be." —Dali Lama

Are you motivated by love? If so, how?

Action Plan & Goals

Love More & Stay in **Balance & Live Fully**.

I commit to:

"He that falls in love with himself will have no rivals."
—Benjamin Franklin

Do you love yourself 100 percent?

Action Plan & Goals

Love More & Stay in **Balance & Live Fully**.

I commit to:

"Keep your eyes wide open before marriage, half shut afterwards." — Benjamin Franklin 1706–1790

Are you critical in your relationships, or can you overlook their flaws?

Action Plan & Goals
Love More & Stay in **Balance & Live Fully**.

I commit to: _____

> "Never have a companion who casts you in the shade."
> —Baltasar Gracian 1601–1658

Do you allow friends who are toxic?

Action Plan & Goals
Love More & Stay in **Balance & Live Fully**.

I commit to:

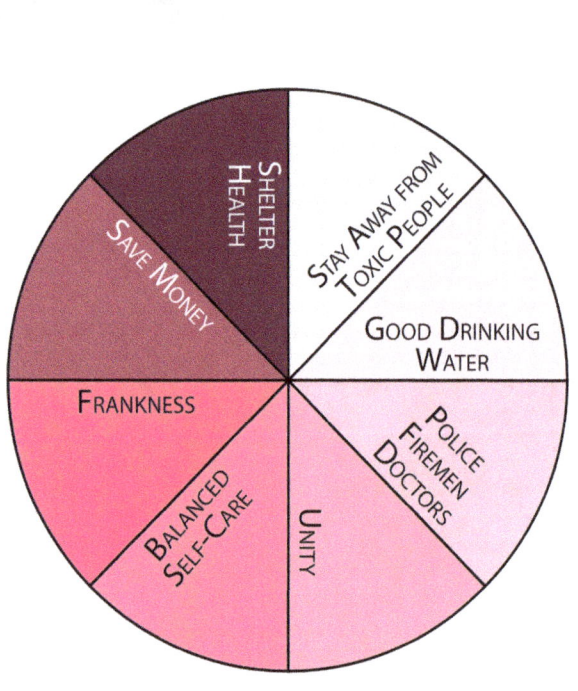

Part 3
Safety & Serenitys

"Move out of your calm. Only grow if you are willing to feel awkward and uncomfortable when you try something new."
—Brian Tracy

How are you getting out of your comfort zone?

Action Plan & Goals

Regarding Safety & Serenity to Stay in **Balance & Live Fully**.

I commit to:

"I learned long ago, never wrestle with a pig. You get dirty, and besides, the pig likes it." —George Bernard Shaw

Are you still trying to fight with unsafe people? It is time to let them go, once and for all.

Action Plan & Goals

Regarding Safety & Serenity to Stay in **Balance & Live Fully**.

I commit to:

"Always forgive your enemies. Nothing annoys them so much." —**Anonymous**

Do you forgive and feel safe?

Action Plan & Goals

Regarding Safety & Serenity to Stay in **Balance & Live Fully**.

I commit to:

> "If we find nothing of interest where we are, we are likely to find little of lasting interest where we wish to go."
> —Edwin Way Teale

Are you content now wherever you are?

Action Plan & Goals

Regarding Safety & Serenity to Stay in **Balance & Live Fully**.

I commit to:

"Non-violence leads to the highest ethics, which is the goal of all evolution. Until we stop harming all other living beings, we are still savages." —Thomas Edison

Are you helping to create a peaceful and safe environment?

Action Plan & Goals

Regarding Safety & Serenity to Stay in **Balance & Live Fully**.

I commit to:

If you're doing the right things. If you're not harming yourself or others. You need not be concerned with what others think. You are free!" —Brian L. Weiss M.D.

What right things are you doing now or want to do?

Action Plan & Goals

Regarding Safety & Serenity to Stay in **Balance & Live Fully**.

I commit to:

"What we anticipate seldom occurs. What we least expected generally happens." —Benjamin Disraeli, Earl of Beaconsfield 1804–1881

Are you feeling Safe and Serene?

Action Plan & Goals
Regarding Safety & Serenity to Stay in **Balance & Live Fully**.

I commit to:

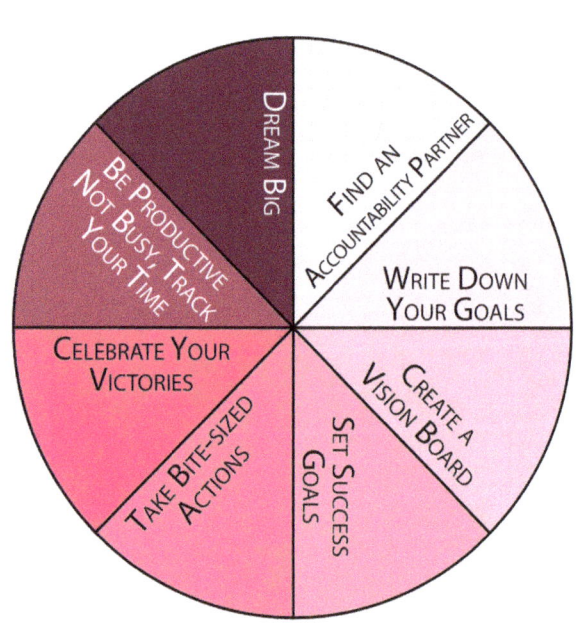

Is your graphic designer not listening to you? Does your book desginer have the experience and skill your book deserves? Are you tired of trying to do it all yourself? Award-winning designer, Ginger Marks, is here to help.

www.DocUmeantDesigns.com

Part 4
Success & Goals

"Our greatest weakness lies in giving up. The most certain way to succeed is always to try just one more time."
—Thomas Edison

What are you willing to try one more time?

Action Plan & Goals

Regarding Success & Goals to Stay in **Balance & Live Fully**.

I commit to:

"Action is the foundational key to all success." —Pablo Picasso

What actions are you willing to take towards your success?

Action Plan & Goals

Regarding Success & Goals to Stay in **Balance & Live Fully**.

I commit to:

"It is your determination and persistence that will make you a successful person." —Kenneth J. Hutchins

What areas are you determined and persistent to get done to be successful?

Action Plan & Goals

Regarding Success & Goals to Stay in **Balance & Live Fully**.

I commit to:

"The act of doing something un-does the fear."
—Shonda Rhimes

What are you afraid of? List actions to overcome your fears. Write down your fears on one side and the opposite on the other side.

Action Plan & Goals

Regarding Success & Goals to Stay in **Balance & Live Fully**.

I commit to:

"Goals are tools for focusing on your life and for inspiring you to take action. Today, determine the worth of your goals . . . because everything you want may not actually be worth having." —Keith D. Harrell

Which goals do you want to keep? Which goals are you willing to release?

Action Plan & Goals

Regarding Success & Goals to Stay in **Balance & Live Fully**.

I commit to:

"Success is a science; if you have the conditions, you get the results." —Oscar Wilde

What plan do you have in place to reach your goals?

Action Plan & Goals
Regarding Success & Goals to Stay in **Balance & Live Fully**.

I commit to:

"Consistency is the last refuge of the unimaginative."
—Oscar Wilde

Do you have a consistent plan for success?

Action Plan & Goals

Regarding Success & Goals to Stay in **Balance & Live Fully**.

I commit to:

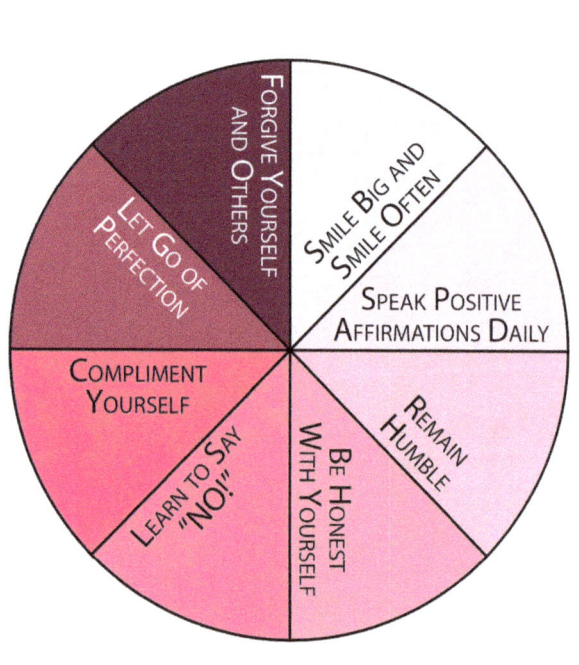

Part 5 Self-Esteem & Self-Love

> "Be yourself; everyone else is already taken."
> —Oscar Wilde

Are you being your true unique authentic self? If not, why not?

Action Plan & Goals

Regarding Self-Esteem & Self-Love. Stay in **Balance & Live Fully**.

I commit to:

"Reconsider a commitment. You have the right to change your mind." —Cheryl Richardson

Do you have a commitment you might want to say no to now?

Action Plan & Goals

Regarding Self-Esteem & Self-Love. Stay in **Balance & Live Fully**.

<u>I commit to:</u>

> "Try to avoid thinking about what you're not: I'm not happy, not rich, not good-looking, and so on. Instead think about what you are: I am joyful, I am prosperous, I am beautiful, and so on. Your self-esteem will rise immeasurably."
> —Sylvia Browne

In what way are you saying nice things about yourself? List your good qualities. How can you change your inner dialogue and self-talk?

Action Plan & Goals

Regarding Self-Esteem & Self-Love. Stay in **Balance & Live Fully**.

I commit to:

"Don't let the perfect be the enemy of good."
—Gretchen Rubin-Voltaire

Is perfectionism holding you back? If so, how?

Action Plan & Goals

Regarding Self-Esteem & Self-Love. Stay in **Balance & Live Fully**.

I commit to:

"If we all did things we are really capable of doing, we would literally astound ourselves." —Thomas Edison

What are you capable of doing that would astound yourself?

www.ingramcontent.com/pod-product-compliance
Lightning Source LLC
Chambersburg PA
CBHW072134070526
44585CB00016B/1677